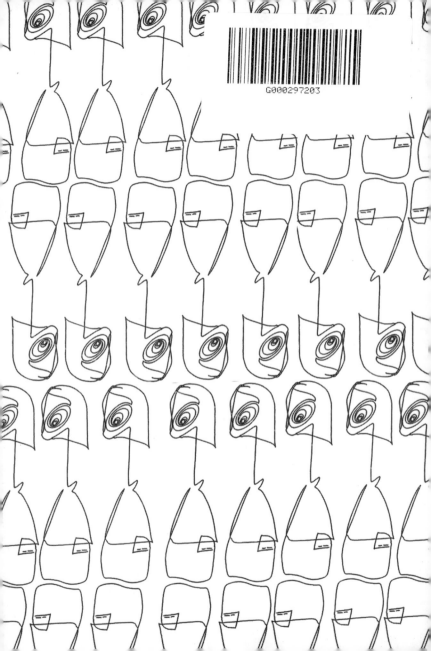

G000297203

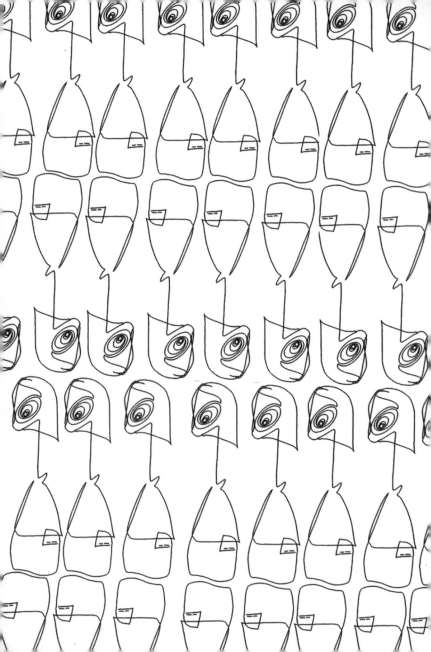

For Ian & Shirley
D.

Apparitions:
a Hurricane

Damian Smyth

Damian Smyth

07·11·13

Templar Poetry

First Published 2012 by Templar Poetry

Fenelon House
Kingsbridge Terrace
58 Dale Road, Matlock, Derbyshire
DE4 3NB
www.templarpoetry.co.uk

ISBN 9781906285869

Typeset by Pliny
Printed and bound in India

"Es mögen wohl Gespenster sein,
Altheidnisch göttlichen Gelichters"
(Heine, from 'Zum Lazarus')

For Bobbie Hanvey

1962

There are still heroes with us every day,
heroes in the old sense, gods and titans.
It's us who've lost the gift and gone away,

forgetting how to know them at a glance
by the cut of a jib, the look in their eye;
it's no wonder they dress down, like buffoons

or derelicts or ghosts, when we pass by.
They don't believe in us. Disguised, blasé,
it's how those strange kings made it home, the Magi.

1963

This is as far from light as you can get:
earth materials such as, in icons,
build the fabric of God, laying facet

over facet, folding the wings of bronze
or gold – egg tempera, gesso, red clay,
bole. And so on. What belongs to the stones

in other words: deadweight of the barony
cut from the very loam with a hatchet,
the whole held fast with a drop of honey.

1964

Again it is the tale of that Chinese jar:
always amove, still turning, on the go,
unfinished; up close or seen from afar,

the figures on it shimmering, aglow,
the pigments crawling through the clay — a hive
of texture seized by itself ages through,

keeping those little gentlemen alive
with honey of the glaze and sweet guitar;
fingers taking a thousand years to move.

1965

Spices docked at Strangford during famine;
florid cargoes: mint, balm of Gilead,
coriander, saffron, waxy lemon

for the Baroness's fat-free pomade,
anise, cinnamon, oil of Araby.
Dark among the dead, the seed of nomad

and rogue swam from Persia and Cuba
like elver through the blood of black semen.
Their sea shanties survive in lullaby.

1966

Even then they were visitors from abroad,
elderly townsfolk; hiding in plain sight
when killings began; but another breed

from the generations that lay in wait.
Tipi women and settled sojourners,
weathered skins made leathery by firelight;

other tongues; possessed of other powers;
wounded, poor, exhausted maraud
-ers; of reticence the last inheritors.

1967

Faces sick in their time. The ague,
biliousness, palsy, atrophy, croup,
measly shin, strangery, impetigo,

quinsy, Bright's disease, ringworm and apop-
-lexy, scarlet rash, lockjaw, milk fever,
chin cough, grocer's itch, edema or drop-

-sy; a goitre like a pouch of silver
coins tied safe at the neck; as out of vogue
as cures, as an ulcer stanched with clover.

1968

When they are first encountered as themselves
— cows — wearing silk skirts of what could be milk
but is that mist near rivers light dissolves

(in childhood that doesn't fear their bulk
just yet but sees pure consciousness up close)
they lean across intimately to talk

of their big bags of lungs, the lips of nos
-trils pulsing at a word like oyster valves,
their atlas hides. Congress with the marvellous.

1969

Tomorrow is Ash Wednesday. I'll wear
the dust on my brow, atone for each time
(there were times) the glamour of the killer

exercised more allure than his victim.
Isn't that the point of the ashy cross?
The frying fish of knowledge burnt the thumb

of Finn MacCool, one of the curios
of myth: that a brutal man might acquire
wisdom while remaining just as callous.

1970

Those dogs that were yellow and white – collies,
dogs with stern faces – you don't see them now.
You don't see the violence when police

go heavy-handed down a narrow lane
like righteous Trojans after Achilles
with his greatcoat and unlicensed shotgun.

His crazed pillage, his dogs like goddesses.
You don't see their big hair, white and yellow,
bloodied locks that had been gold like Lassie's.

1971

All but him had died in the blaze,
flames kicking the doors of the bedrooms in
and letting themselves out by the windows,

piggy-backing on the backs of children,
while he was sliding up the banisters
uselessly, hand over fist. The rowan

she'd planted was still smouldering for hours
after they had recovered the bodies.
He wears a glove on his missing fingers.

1972

It used to be, when they coated the balls
with cellulose nitrate, the merest kiss
was enough to blow holes in the tables.

Those sweating globes in an Indian mess.
Years in the Raj, the chaps could take their pick:
drinks on the verandah, barrack largesse;

the pink memsahibs no longer homesick;
all easy in a world without rebels.
But even safety shots still packed a kick.

1973

Out at Rossglass, what there is of a beach
is broken crockery, rolled in from ships
foundered years ago. No two fragments match.

However small the bits, not one escapes
the obsessive collection for the sands
the sea is at and which it never stops,

so when there are shards that shine like diamonds,
it could be the engagement ring or some such
of that girl whose bomb went off in her hands.

1974

Poems talk to each other over time
even those that don't know whose they are
or whose tongue they've been implicated in.

Like one's own face in dialogue
with earlier versions, captured, also true.
There was a blackbird singing on the roof

and somewhere else one other in reply,
as if it was itself, its memory,
and it pausing, puzzled, then quizzing it.

1975

Don't be so wrong as to think this is ab
-out something, stories of an oddity,
a freak or inmate picking at a scab;

events in real time or things of beauty
rendered or worried at like a taboo;
the world of people in all their sweaty

exactitude; as if that were more true
than whatever it is that can describe
that wood pigeon's call ripe as an oboe.

1976

Years after, he still goes up to the site
of his vision in the Dromara hills,
alone among all of them no misfit

or devotee; the Rosary's knuckles
wrapped in his own adding every
detail of a hedgeful of bicycles

to the pure fact of that discovery
he'd lit upon, secret and recondite:
House of Gold, O Tower of Ivory.

1977

Seagulls inland, a monastic penance.
They meditate over the Asylum
where storms miles off still trouble the curtains.

They are on their own. It is the custom
of their kind to muster where there is quiet
air, but each alone is just as far from home.

Down below, among the untidy allot
-ments, which are all that's left of the patients,
the roses they'd looked after run riot.

1978

If I turn my eyes away for a minute,
in the way of things – a child at play,
grass growing – next I know an intimate,

just now a friend, just dead, gets in the way.
So much for wildlife and the cute botanists'
gentle poems of gewgaws, slick antennae.

They are appalling, uninvited guests.
Dead girls are the worst, loved at first sight:
drowned smocks, pondlife hair, scarry turquoise wrists.

1979

I think sometimes it was myself that died
ages ago and it's me is the ghost;
or sometimes that it is these shapes instead

are the apparitions of those who lost,
a bonfire of poems by Heinrich Heine
or a plate with the head of John the Baptist.

In any case, they march through my brain
each night, my folk, battering my blood,
vexed like a procession of Orangemen.

1980

At ninety-one, the only thing he had
to anticipate was a painful case
of last things. Nothing occurred. Instead,

it was a good death of consummate grace,
such a passing into ease from boredom
his one child could ascribe it to caprice,

facing into old age himself solemn
-ly, finding himself stunned by a bedside
and bereft and not sure when or by whom.

1981

My granny said "You'd wonder how they're trained"
when Bugs and Daffy Duck came on: appalled
at their neck, their mouthiness, their harebrained

antics in her own house. They couldn't be killed.
With the TV off or a channel hopped,
they'd still be there; in hiding, just parolled

from seen to unseen, screwball and unstopped
by her striking at them when she was blind
with the *Irish News*, the chairlegs walloped.

1982

As soon as he went down across the baize,
as soon as, there was a power like voodoo:
intensity, hypnosis of a gaze

fixed along the full length of a cue
as if there were a kind of experiment
underway, of artifice or taboo,

as if, unless he controlled the ancient
charm geometry had wasted on ashtrays,
Aaron's rod would collapse like a serpent.

1983

Really it can't be emphasised enough:
there is no moral. In *Peau de Chagrin*,
Balzac describes a tablecloth of snow,

a napkin with a bread roll like a crown.
"I wanted throughout my youth," said Cézanne,
"to paint that tablecloth." Later he'd know

that if he balanced and shaded without strain
rolls and napkins and left the rest alone,
gold would just arrive, with snow new fallen.

1984

This is by way of a *missa brevis*
for the Workhouse and the Asylum dead.
Laid to rest with neither song nor service,

those souls drawn up in a silken thread
from under the fields, rushlights, bog cotton,
to light here, visible, fixed, defeated,

now their names are to be said or written
for the first time to charm the old disgrace.
Writ in stone or wind; or almost written.

1985

Even when it's tough there are nice touches
in a life as rough as a badger's arse:
five children by three separate bitches

and he's breeding rose-leaves in different colours;
behaving like a gallant or aesthete,
dusting pollen on stigmas with horsehairs.

A delicacy of sorts. A retreat
from disappointment; a penance, which is
those children cutting him dead in the street.

1986

I do have a place where I am at home.
There is a country with so many trees
– oak, yew, cypress – hum of an aerodrome,

violets nodding their heads with heavy bees.
A vision. It kisses with the lover's
language of the nation's old enemies,

English. The way English endeavours
to say 'I love you' and delivers
what it says, so much lovelier each time.

1987

Belonging's not as easy as it looks.
Birth's in the middle of it, yes; annulled
by suffering, unrepaired by antiques,

mementoes, pedigrees; is ridiculed
anyway as a passport to the tribes.
Once it was enough to be 'well travelled'

to be forgiven the honeybees'
homewardness. But I'll be fished off the rocks
after death, two eyes glassy as goosegabs.

1988

That part-time soldier shot at Ardpatrick
was a coalman. At Tyrella watch-house,
on the very coast the *Great Britain* struck,

coal's rolled along the seabed without fuss
for centuries, shoreward, steady, covert,
the sea remaking it light as pumice,

porous as bones, close as a human heart.
Suffering done, it keeps a new alert,
warm to the touch and rough as a handshake.

1989

I am staking my claim to a country.
Its population sober and dying.
I've drawn myself maps, an inventory

of useless artefacts, discarded, fraying,
broken, strange, with natural features
of progressively intensifying

anonymity. I will brook no chairs
at shop-fronts nor have the effrontery
to tolerate coloraturas.

1990

What country is it? The river's altered
in summer, setting down its warm wide flanks
among the islands, placid as a herd

of charolais; heads of foam on the banks
from a mild turbulence under the bridge;
rich woods done in water with different inks;

a thousand swans. The heart's last anchorage
before seasons change and memory's soured.
One kind of Ireland, an unsafe knowledge.

1991

Near where they chose to build the cinema
there was a shrine already with its ghost,
in a field, 'a very Aceldama'.

A young man had been gunned down in his guts.
Above the heads of children in the stalls,
the light lays with a painter's hand its gouts

of colour carefully, making murals
with its own self as if it was stigma
-tic, weeping on bandages shapes like angels'.

1992

I am listening to death, its noises;
for all the tales are stories of decay,
of fading light, of falling leaves; pauses

in the music arthritic fingers play
plucking the sheets in an emptying ward.
The fox has bent his tracks in the barley

or something has, for sure against the grain.
The shouts are loud. The bay window closes,
the fierce glass ballooning like a membrane.

1993

Jimmy Nick-Nick turned up with thirty knives
in a 'leather' box with a 'silver' hasp
- *there's even three for cheese.* Of all the spivs

the most winsome, the riskiest, most wasp
-waisted, a pool-hall dude; a maverick
surviving hand-to-mouth on the cusp

of bye-ball and murder, with no stomach
for death. But he's in one of those lost graves
some one of us will stumble on, dumbstruck.

1994

Heifers' lungs banging in the dusk like drums.
Inside cows, it is all motive and slick,
the sound of underwater museums,

gaudy light filtering on each relic
suspended in its veiny vat of blood.
They pray prostrate like saints; are angelic

charmers consistently misunderstood,
both substance of their god and His pilgrims,
praise shrunk to one word and that one bellowed.

1995

There was an alarm ringing in the distance.
The old lady's yellow roses were black
in the blue and red lamps of the ambulance,

and there were the slow bells of the lilac,
still rolling on the night path from the sleeve
of the policeman who kicked in the lock,

her tiny resort of mint and foxglove
rushed by professionals, those big footprints
on a rug stuck with aniseed and clove.

1996

After the races, the stand's desertion;
dockets blown about, stubs along the rails,
the track gouged by the horses' exertion

and at the third from home those blue sails
of canvas screens mounted on a tripod
mean the faller's still down, kicking his heels,

for the *coup de grâce*. Thus Magnus Barfod,
Norseman and king — at least in one version —
waited for the axe, waist-deep in mud.

1997

Mr Stockdale brought turnip and apple
to the editor's office and left them
for the edification of people:

freak growths, swollen tubers, the odd legume
native to these parts but uniquely scarred,
shaped like a thing the wind would exhume

from the Stockdale vault in the old graveyard
at Ballyculter. Pine under maple.
And then his own obituary appeared.

1998

What I brought to the city, to Belfast,
was Struell water, smuggled in phials.
A wound-healer, eye-doctor; a Baptist

on the way with secular cordials,
digs to digs, sprinkling the pure unguent
on college stairwells; clattery hobnails.

Comfort food. Each anointing an event
like the Latter-Day Saints secretly christ
-ening through polling lists the ignorant.

1999

Nowhere else. It is always worrying,
the absolute loneliness of the light
-house: existential, real though it is a thing,

its bitterness spent on every climate.
Being built is no bar to the common
disdain objects share for their desperate

purposes: practice shots by the gunman,
deadly secrets, raw wounds without bleeding;
struck staring the sun down like a gnomon.

2001

It is always All Souls' Night at the coast;
for all the dead the lighthouse keeps vigil,
lifting up its torch at this last outpost

of everything strenuous and fragile.
For example, the *Georgetown Victory*'s
sunk still shiny like a lunar module,

buried in sand remote as a prairie's.
Another fury the barony missed;
another brilliance; another country's.

2002

And then the rain falls; and I know that if
it's raining in the town it's dry out there,
along the coast, by Ardglass and Kilclief,

with the rocks burning black beyond repair.
The roads hold the tide by the aerodrome,
cups of salt water for the traveller

who has taken the longest route back home,
through air and earth and fire after take-off
in that order. The rain drops like a psalm.

2003

They buried us with what were to become
'grave goods' – a designation arrived at
only after, for things in the meantime

still useful, simple, in love or combat:
a Claddagh ring, football scarves, a nose-stud,
snaps unglued from a family album

and tucked still sticky along the smooth wood;
a cellphone the screaming grandkids were let
hide charged up in the folds on silent mode.

2004

Daffodils in the graveyard, and cypress,
yew, organic paraphernalia.
There will be those drawn to this place

or not on occasion: then those daily
tending to earth itself, making good loss
with poppy, lily; the regalia

of paramilitaries and police
observing on one site, unhappily,
the least contentious, most enduring truce.

2005

He died under artificial light,
a shotgun muzzle pressed to his own chin
so hard it described a figure of eight

as if something had laid eggs on his skin.
Marksmen and cameramen alike blinked
at him through lenses which drew them close in

to his small constellation of instinct
driven to ground like a meteorite;
at bay and safely lifeless. Then he winked.

2006

No thing more animal, that clarinet,
though what – before it lay down in its suede
pouches fore and aft a perfect fit

as if that had been its scarlet flesh, sloughed
off and become plush as the bones lacquer –
it was, is unknown in its solitude

now my father's dead, now in a reliquar
-y of his own who could make sense of it
like Aaron, rod and staff, serpent-waker.

2007

Only after I'd been to John Doris,
optometrist – middle-aged bar mitzvah –
and the wares of his manufactories

(slit lamps, phoropters, all the univer
-sal laws of perspective newly minted,
valid for the quick as the cadaver)

did I come to see a world fog-haunted
return strict and bizarre as Portaferry's
covetous tides, untaken for granted.

2008

The tulip had filled up with snow and bent
right over with it and broken its neck.
Everywhere else it was so gentle,

even leaving, with each other bloom racked
up on the windowsill, a bleached blonde bouffant.
But where it found the one that was weak,

it had been merciless, by accident,
piling onto it its delicate stack
of almost nothingness like an earthquake.

2009

I'd rather be wrong and on his side
than right and on yours. Outlaws always win
even when they lose; but it's a landslide

when they win, tears and snatters and a grin
as wide as Sandy Row, any pretext
for a drink in style, much to the chagrin

of those who'd hate them in any context,
dead or alive. As Dickie Davis said
Hue and cry one week, song and dance the next.

2010

Wells of stone can't hold the water within
though that's what their walls are for, purpose-built
to trammel urgency with discipline,

channel it, but leave the sweetness unspoilt.
Elsewhere in the grounds, though, the cure blossoms
underfoot in spite of violence, spilt

by the gentle earth from brackish fathoms,
so what occurs surprisingly's still in
that universe of failed events: poems.

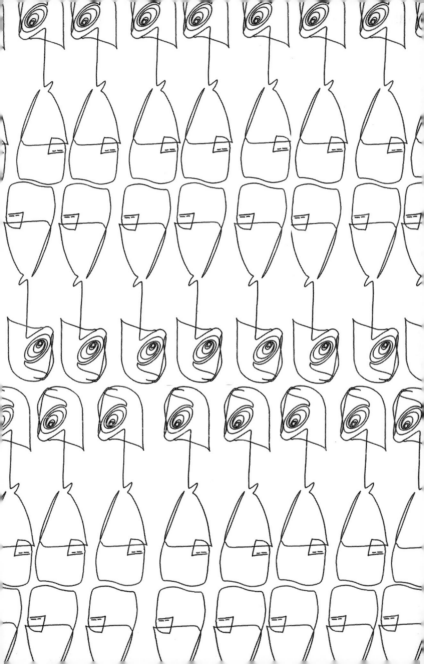

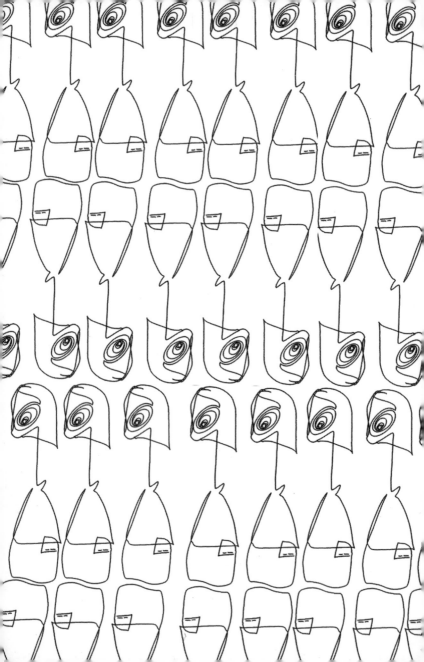